OUT OF EDEN

LORCA'S VERMONT POETRY

BY

SEAN ANDREW HEANEY

SIMON & WHITE TRANSLATION

2015

Thanks to the Vermont Community Foundation of Arts & Literature. In Newport, Voc/Micro Business of VT, Jody Casey & Amy Robinson, the staff of the Goodrich Memorial Library; special thanks to Toni Croteau. At Passumpsic Savings Bank, Jeannie Pray. Whipple's Studio & Christian Kerner. Alice Wellinger for her cover painting; "Lorca as St. Sebastian." Farrar, Straus & Giroux for the Simon & White translation of poems from Federico Garcia-Lorca's "Poet In New York," 2nd Revised edition. Special thanks to Christopher Maurer, Laura Garcia-Lorca & The Lorca Foundation, Madrid, Spain. Deepest thanks to Gretchen E. Lewis & Tree Swenson. And especially to Denise Piette of The Front Desk Office Supplies, editor, proof reader, and friend. Semper Fi.

Copyright © 2015

All rights reserved

Printed in the United States of America

LIBRARY OF CONGRESS
CATALOGING-IN-PUBLICATION DATA

Heaney, Sean A..
Out of Eden: Lorca's Vermont Poetry / Sean Andrew Heaney

ISBN 9781936711475

10 9 8 7 6 5 4 3 2 1

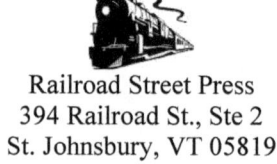

Railroad Street Press
394 Railroad St., Ste 2
St. Johnsbury, VT 05819

This book is dedicated to the memories of
Joseph P. Heaney, Sr., and Joseph P. Heaney, Jr.,
And to the memory of Liam Rector, Poet, Mentor
and Free Speech Advocate.

A dead man in Spain is more alive when dead than anywhere else on earth.

> Federico Garcia-Lorca

Initium ................................................................................................................. 1

Eden, VT March 2015 ........................................................................................ 1

Chapter One: The Spanish Prisoner ….....………………………………………3

Chapter Two: METROPOLIS …............................................................................9

Chapter Three: The American Friend ..................................................................12

IV
POEMS OF LAKE EDEN MILLS ......................................................................16

VI
INTRODUCTION TO DEATH ..........................................................................19
*(Poems of Solitude in Vermont)*

Chapter Four: Notes on The Poems ....................................................................31

Chapter Five: The Depression & Paradise Regained ..………………………..36

Chapter Six: Last Act/Last August ......................................................................37

Chapter Seven: The Unreliable Narrator & The Rogue Scholar .......................40

Chapter Eight: Garcia-Lorca, Martyr & Saint Innocent:
                  Found in Translation ....................................................45

Bibliography ........................................................................................................47

Initium

Adam & Eve.
The serpent cracked
the mirror
in a thousand pieces,
& the apple
Was his rock.
F G-L



LAKE EDEN, VERMONT, March, 2015

The Ides have come and gone and it still feels like snow. The skies are sullen gray over the lake's black waters that almost break at my feet on the narrow way in front of the red wood shingled summer cottage. On the clapboards of the porch there is a brass Vermont Historical Landmark plaque.

The raised gold leaf letters catch the sun's brief cameo and the dedication reads, not to some soldier or statesman, but to Spain's greatest modern poet, Federico Garcia-Lorca. In August, 1929, he was in residence and wrote poetry that would appear in his magnum opus, "Poet In New York."

The pastoral mid-section of the poem consists of poems written in Vermont, here, at a friend's summer camp in Eden Mills, and those written at a fellow poet's ramshackle farm house in New York State. The poetry was not a celebration of Nature after a season in the concrete jungle of New York City, but a watershed in the middle of the work that captured nothing less than the Dark Night of the Soul for Garcia-Lorca, and the reckoning that would follow. Seven years later, Garcia-Lorca would leave the manuscript of his epic poem on his editor's desk, with a note that concluded with ". . . I'll be back tomorrow." He would never see that day, or his poem into print. In August, 1936, the Spanish Civil War had begun. He was dragged from a "Safe" house and sometime between dawn and noonday, executed by Franco's Nationalist guard. His body has never been found.

From that crucial summer of 1929 in Vermont to the final day on his native soil, his fame and prestige as both a poet and a playwright had made him a charismatic figure in the literary world and in high society. Neither his work nor the open secret of his homosexuality seemed a danger to him. One more circumspect would have seen that the nature of his writing, especially the plays, and his brushes with notoriety in public and private, were not lost on a deeply conservative and faith based culture that was, and is, Spain.

The adage, "The child is the father of the man," was never more apt than when applied to Federico Garcia Lorca. For an artist of unique discernment and sensitivity, he also retained a child-like naiveté coupled with a certain braggadocio that was part of his charm. This charm and the tenacity of his trust in others was to prove fatal to him.

Lake Eden looks much the same today as it did in August, 1929. It has avoided the exploitation and "development" of many of Vermont's other recreation areas. It remains a secret garden; not hiding from the world, but well hidden. The cottage is locked up and on the market for a quarter of a million. It is off-season for "The Summer People," as the natives refer to the vacationers from out-of-town. Looking at the corner of the porch where Garcia-Lorca and his friend, Philip Cummings, were photographed in their workspace and where they slept in adjacent hammocks, or through the windows at the sheet shrouded furniture, it seems less an Eden than a Paradise Lost. If the Poet's ten day stay didn't shake the world, the part of his work accomplished here would reverberate with aftershocks that can still be felt decades later, when his poem finally found translators that would at last bequeath the book in style to the English speaking world.

As for most of the previous translations of Garcia-Lorca, the poet Roy Campbell would quip:

> "Not only did he lose his life
> By shots assassinated:
> But with a hammer and a knife
> Was after that – translated."

~ ~ ~

> "When the worm turned
> He learned
> This apple is a
> Blood filled tear..."
>
> Jim Carroll

Chapter One

**The Spanish Prisoner**

Granada's favorite son had done himself proud. At the Residencia in Madrid, two years shy of thirty, Federico Garcia-Lorca was widely considered Spain's best young poet and it's most promising. Along with his close friends, Salvador Dali and Luis Bunuel, whose later achievements in their vocations as painter and filmmaker would bring them worldwide fame, it was a formidable graduating class.

Garcia-Lorca could be forgiven if he felt that he and Dali were somewhat ahead of Bunuel in tangible achievement, on the stage and the printed page. His second play, "Marina Pineda," with sets by Dali, was a major hit at it's opening in Barcelona in 1927. The following year, his book, "Gypsy Ballads," was both a critical and popular success.

Apart from the true poet's gift of being able to make himself miserable in the hour of fame, in 1928 Garcia-Lorca confessed to being near suicide in his state of depression. His saving grace was also the gift of the true poet, the ability to create, regardless of material or geographical surroundings, extremes of emotion or the opinions of others, be they friends, enemies, strangers or family. It would serve him well, especially in the years to come.

A fellow poet had called him, "a solitary who couldn't bear solitude." To most of his contemporaries he appeared as a creative dynamo, always at the center of singing, storytelling or artistic debate. His nature was kind and generous, and he had the unique ability to make fellow students and artists feel he was a friend who could be counted on in personal matters, or in his evaluation of their work. Any writer will acknowledge the latter as a rare quality indeed.

While this side of his personality was not entirely a false face, it is a tribute to his strength of character that he was able to wear a masque to cover what then would have been considered the deviant half of his persona. The poet's despair was a negative self image, the duende, or the daemonic inscape of Death in Life that Garcia-Lorca maintained was present in all great Art, especially in Spain. In a country whose favorite public spectacle is the ceremonial Danza de la Muerte of bullfighting, it is hard to argue the point.

For the homosexual, in that time and place, same-sex relationships, if brought to light, would result in a similar public suicide in the social arena. Regardless of his other virtues and achievements, being a homosexual was against the laws of God and Man in his native land, where a good family name is paramount, and a hyper-masculinity, machismo, is respected.

The anguish bedeviling Garcia-Lorca in 1927 and '28 was both personal and professional, which for him was one and the same. He, Dali and Bunuel had experimented with Surrealism in their art, partially as a reaction to the middle class conventions and strictures of Church and State. Only with Dali can one say that if Surrealism hadn't existed that it would have been necessary for the painter to invent it. If the layman recognizes it at all today, it is in the masterworks of this artist.
For novice filmmaker Luis Bunuel, the misogynist and misanthrope in him liked anything that was an offense to middle class or religious values. The integrity of his vision, refined and refocused in relative obscurity, would grant him fame in his golden years when most filmmakers are looking at their career in retrospect. He would continue to employ oneiric and surrealist imagery in his later films. His brilliant images and his wicked satire were employed as master strokes of the maestro up to his Academy award winning best foreign film, "The Discreet Charm of the Bourgeoisie" in 1972.

It is fair to say that Garcia-Lorca put the most faith in opinions of his work that came from Bunuel and Dali, his two best friends. To them, his "Gypsy Ballads," were an affront to the Modern, according to whatever highly perishable manifesto usually goes along with a new movement in the Arts. Not recognizing themselves as conforming non-conformists, Bunuel and Dali now doubled down on the odd man out, and accused Garcia-Lorca of pillaging folk art, pandering to tourist notions of local color. For his part, Garcia-Lorca would never acknowledge himself as a Surrealist, even at his most surreal. He was simpatico with what Raymond Radiguet, protégé of Jean Cocteau, had to say about the contention between different schools of Art and class prejudice: "It is not enough to attack the bourgeois; one must go further, and attack the Avant-Garde!"

Garcia-Lorca was born into a rich cultural and spiritual tradition, and far from rejecting his legacy, he sought out in the works of the past from Spain's diverse cultures what resonated with his own artistic sensibility. "The Gypsy Ballads," were not superficial artistic poaching, and gained a new pitch from their Arabic origins through Garcia-Lorca's modern adaptations.

He had no intention of limiting his influences, ancient or modern, to follow the vogue, be it a rogue wave like Surrealism or the established popular culture and its middle class mores.

Garcia-Lorca was prescient in seeing the limitations of any school or movement, but the contempt of his two best friends cut to the quick. At one with this criticism was Dali distancing himself from what, for five years, had been a Romantic friendship; at least for Federico. The two had been comrades-in-art since they met, each incorporating the other into their various modes of creation, refining and debating artistic theory in any medium, and even engaging in some the morbid performance piece theatrics, like Garcia-Lorca playing the dead bullfighter being carried through the streets in all his funereal finery. Dali would incorporate the figure or face of the Poet into his drawings. Correspondence between the two was often illustrated with sketches by Dali and the more childlike drawings of Garcia-Lorca.

Both had written essays or prose poems about the figure of St. Sebastian, in and out of his place in Christian artwork. Bound and executed by arrows for being a Christian while a member of the Roman Legion, and for converting two fellow soldiers, he rose above his suffering, not renouncing the New Faith. Artist's renderings of his nobility and angelic passivity bordering on the ecstatic in execution, not unlike the noble death of the gored bullfighter, had been the subject of debate since his martyrdom had first become a popular subject for artists commissioned by the Church. His passion, captured in marble or painted altarpiece, was, to Dali and Garcia-Lorca, a perfect abstract of the theory of negative capability; joy and stoicism in the hour of pain balanced and raised to the level of spiritual ecstasy. Their writings on the Saint, as well as his influence on the later works of Yukio Mishima and Tennessee Williams, helped canonize St. Sebastian as a Gay icon.

The intensity of their life and work together made Garcia-Lorca think Dali had at least come to terms with his sexuality in the way that he himself had, as a winding together like the DNA of spiritual and carnal love, the sacred and profane as a new Sacrament. To make what was considered transgressive a supernatural consummation or communion to spite the Catholic Church was, in the event, much more daring than embracing or rejecting Surrealism.

Dali, who in his appearance and manner seemed to be so Gay he couldn't even think Straight, went into homosexual panic. He rejected Garcia-Lorca's overture, compounded it by criticizing his popular book of poems and finally by throwing in his lot with the macho Bunuel. Bunuel had already given Garcia-Lorca the third degree about his sexuality after some of his other friends had referred to the esteemed poet as, "The queer in the bowtie." The three did not part as friends. For Bunuel and Dali, rejection of the

poet for his sexual preference was also a good way to disguise their jealousy of Garcia-Lorca's rapid maturity as an artist and the recognition that he received for it. This would have been even greater if Garcia-Lorca hadn't been reluctant to publish his poetry. He was superstitious about seeing his printed poems "dead on the page."
This attitude would have much to do with his preference, in the coming years, for watching his poetic plays "come alive" on the stage. He discovered that being a popular playwright was much more gratifying than the status of respected poet.

Of the Triumvirate, Dali had the most gargantuan appetite for fame. In later days he seemed to be more interested in his cult of celebrity once his work had achieved respect and/or notoriety. Often painting himself into his own paintings, he wanted to be the Seer AND the Seen. He ended up creating a public persona as bizarre as any of his paintings or writings, and while still capable of producing a masterpiece at any stage of his long career, his Superstar status was always up front, even when it became as vacuous as that of his bastard child in the Arts, Andy Warhol.

But much of the above was in the future and of no solace to Garcia-Lorca in his then agony of unrequited love. He tried to put a brave face on it at first, taking up with a young and callow sculptor, Emilio Soriano Aladren. He made him a protégé, introducing him to established authors and people in his mileau who he thought might be of help to the aspiring artist. Aladren took what was offered him, but lest Garcia-Lorca have any ideas of a quid pro quo for services rendered, he then rounded on him, rebuking him publicly, while playing down the connections made and influence of the senior writer.

To put paid to Garcia-Lorca's pratfalls and humiliation in his relationships after their parting, Dali married the woman who would be the muse of and in his painting, Galina, one of the first models to be known by her first name alone as Dali would be by his last. His chief attraction seemed to be callipygian, her well-rounded buttocks inspiring many paintings like "Virgin Auto-Sodomized by Her own Chastity". It made some of his written remarks on his parting with Lorca seem disingenuous, at the very least. Bunuel and Dali then gave birth to the first Surrealist films, L'Age d'Or and Un Chien Andalou (An Andalusian Dog).Together with the persistent memory of Dali's melting watches, the latter sixteen minute film is the other best known curio of Spanish surrealism. A fever dream fetish with repetition of images and non-sequiters, a Buster Keaton-like figure is thwarted in his erotic pursuits while a doomed couple assault and ravish each other only to be doomed to the fatality of being half buried, just out of each other's reach. A sensation in the artistic coteries where it was shown, Garcia-Lorca intuitively took it to be a satire at his expense. Today, the opening image of the razored eyeball's split vision and the man pulling a piano by a rope with a rotting donkey splayed over the keys (Gypsy Ballad, anyone?) still holds its shock value for the uninitiated. The film is more a very specific cinematic period piece, valued for the Bunuel & Dali shooting script prose poem and the montage of Bunuel's imagery. Back then, the Surrealist stag reel was the last straw for the Andulasian poet and the two men he once called friends.

Garcia-Lorca the extrovert and bon vivant disappeared. As had happened before, the Poet went into seclusion to try to reconcile his divided self with his personal and artistic aspirations. Ernest Hemingway, who would put a double barreled "AMEN" to his own life, had once noted that only the writer and the suicide know true loneliness. The American, who also loved Spain, the bullfight and the juice of the vine, would have known Garcia-Lorca's play and theory of duende on the most intimate terms. He called bouts of depression, "The Black Dog," from which the only way to survive was to come to terms with it. To try to take arms against it was futile; It must run it's course and be reconciled to one's life and work.

Fortunately, not all of Garcia-Lorca's friends were self-serving and disloyal. Once a depressive can be reached, a true friend is like a ministering angel. Federico was twice blessed with a loving family, although there is reason to believe that the last two incidents in his life had gained some currency, and that the Poet himself was beginning to fire back at those he felt had deserted him. Word may have gotten back to his family, and this may have been the occasion of his official coming out party, or a confirmation of what they had known but would not believe.

At this juncture, there seemed to be nothing for it but a change of backdrop for Garcia-Lorca. His friend, Fernando de los Rios, was about to sail to the United States for a lecture tour and asked that the Poet be his travelling companion. Garcia-Lorca had never been abroad. Although somewhat apprehensive of leaving for a foreign country when he had no English, he remembered an American academic prodigy, Philip Cummings, with whom he had become acquainted with at the Residencia. The young man, fluent in Spanish, had offered his services as guide and translator should he ever come to the States. Garcia-Lorca had long felt obliged to make an effort to learn English for the translation of his plays & poetry to gain international recognition, and now on his way to New York, decided that Columbia University would be congenial to his studies. Cummings had spoken to him of a family summer camp in the wilds of Vermont that might provide a break from the city heat.

In June of 1929, Garcia-Lorca embarked on a voyage of discovery and a flight from disgrace and regret. As he boarded The Olympia, sister ship on the White Star line to the Titanic, he might have recognized the mixed auguries had he been less wrapped up in himself. Nothing could have prepared him for the New York City experience, except his viewing of Fritz Lang's futuristic film of modern utopia and dystopia, "Metropolis." The silent classic was made by Lang after his first visit to New York. Even if he had been a prophet, Garcia-Lorca surely never would have believed that he had only seven years of life left to capture his new experiences and visions in poetry and plays, or the cataclysm his native land would be subject to in the not too distant future. The provincial poet was about to become the narrator-voyager of his own Divine Comedy, who begins midway through the journey of life finding himself in the dark, physically and spiritually.

> The dawn was putting the Statue of Liberty out;
> That torch of hers, you know——
> I started walking home across the Bridge . . .
> 
> Cutty Sark/The Bridge
> Hart Crane.

Chapter Two

**METROPOLIS**

Sailing into the New World, New York City harbor has been a portal of dreams for immigrants from every country in the Old World, the huddled masses moving in bag and baggage by the light of the statue of the Great Goddess, Liberty.

It is not known at what particular moment Federico Garcia-Lorca began to hold Gotham in fear and loathing. He had brought the duende with him, like smoke and spilt wine on his clothes with a chip off the Old World on one shoulder, and a stained glass chip on the other. He did not articulate his feelings to his hosts, the Spanish speaking intelligentsia of the city. Nor would his thoughtful, colorful correspondence with his family betray the tone and content of the poetry he was composing, freely and with a prophet's violent revelations. New York City, the hero of so much Modern poetry, became Garcia-Lorca's most daunting antagonist. He would have to find new forms and madder music to capture this, and what he found would make "Poet In New York" distinctive from his entire canon. This was true then, and ten years later, in 1940, when first translated into English. That year, the time, as well as the translations and critical interpretations, were out-of-tune.

He must have been uncomfortable in the dormitories and class rooms of Columbia University. His attendance record for his English class bears this out. He was never keen to learn the language of his host country, especially with so much pleasure and distraction off campus. He was fortunate indeed to have the friendship and experience of the Spanish speaking community, some of whom he knew from back in Spain. Their guidance made sure the Poet saw what was worth seeing, and more. That remains the only fair description of New York City: Good, Bad and Ugly, it has MORE of everything than any city in the world. The visitor had also better pick up the pace to stay in step with the fast moving swing of things.

His friends also made certain he wasn't taken for a country cousin, however much he might look the part in his heavy tweeds, knickerbockers, knee socks and clod hoppers. He was taken to the theater and to see and hear the new talking pictures, where he claimed he learned more English than at college. His guides took him to hear the best music being played in Harlem, and of all his diversions, this music and the people who played it and crowded the clubs to hear it, made the most profound impression on him. He went to the great museums of New York City to view the Old Masters. He also went to services at a Russian Catholic Orthodox Church, and to temple for Spanish Jews, Shearith Israel synagogue. These visits served to confirm him in his Spanish Catholicism, a devotion to the Faith he was born in to. Of course, these were letters to his family. To his friends and in his poetry, he could be vociferously anti-Catholic, because the Church had failed its mission to help the poor, and his sexuality made him anathema.

His imitations of the lives and deaths of the Saints were satire as only a former member of the choir could write; his fantastical Ode To The Most Blessed Sacrament was a scandal to his Catholic mentors, and never finished, or perhaps abandoned, though at the time he told a friend it was the best poem he had ever written.

Here is perhaps the most useful way to read the volume that would become "Poet In New York." Not until the first bilingual edition by Greg Simon and Steven F. White, edited by Christopher Maurer in 1988 could the reader balance the letters home with the poetry he was writing during his stay in America. Garcia-Lorca's life was a performance, and he was a fair judge of what audience he was playing to. That does not mean that his experiences related in his correspondence completely contradicted his poetry of the same time and place. Maybe the best autobiography of the Poet is a side-by-side reading of these two divergent recordings of his life as a man and an artist. The reader can see just what a fabulist with the people, places and poems of his journey Garcia-Lorca could be in the lecture and poetry reading he gave in Madrid in 1932, that concludes the $2^{nd}$ revised edition of "Poet In New York." Before the publication of the first edition, which he always dreaded, and, in the event, would never live to see, Garcia-Lorca read the poems and provided the back story of their creation. He wouldn't bore himself or his audience with anything like the journalistic truth. The yarns he spun between the readings of the poems were colorful, horrible and fantastic, and had only passing glances with the real genesis of the poetry. This reading as re-creation was highly entertaining, and, often times, a superior version of the facts. It was theatrical, more like a stage reading of a play. It is indicative of where the Poet's interests were leading him; to his best years as a dramatist.

Of the writers and artists Garcia-Lorca was to meet in the City, none is more fascinating, and frustrating for the reader, than his introduction to the great American poet, Hart Crane. Crane was just finishing his epic poem, "The Bridge," the antithesis of what "Poet In New York," would become, using the Brooklyn Bridge as a massive Aeolian harp to play the lyric/ epic story of America and "lend a myth to God." Contrary aims, but alike in ambition and scope, this was perhaps the only instance where the reader rues the fact that Crane had little Spanish and Garcia-Lorca less English. Both would claim Walt Whitman as their literary forbearer and homosexual pioneer in their epic poems, though bringing him to the modern age would pose some difficulties; more than kin and less than kind.

Going to see Crane in his rooms at 130 Columbia Heights in Brooklyn, Garcia-Lorca and his friend, Angel Flores, found him in his element; drunk as a lord and hosting a crew of equally besotted sailors. Garcia-Lorca's friend excused himself, leaving him to a seafood dinner with great lashings of scotch whiskey, the two poets communicating their enthusiasms in the universal tongue: drunkenness. Crane had long used alcohol to melt any inhibitions he might have regarding his own homosexuality. Like Garcia-Lorca, he was tormented by demons and daemons, and after years of heavy drinking and rough trade, marked by intervals of unrivaled creativity, the Devil was overdue. Crane was a suicide two years after "The Bridge," proved only moderately successful in its debut. Though their one meeting was a bacchanal that Crane probably didn't remember and Garcia-Lorca couldn't forget, the meeting of the two is in the chronology of the collected works and biographies of both poets. Crane's chronology would end first, in 1932, with Garcia-Lorca's final reckoning only five years later.

### Adam

Adam dreams in the fever of the clay
Of a child who comes galloping
Through the double pulse of his cheek.

But a dark other Adam is dreaming
a neuter moon of seedless stone
where the child of light will burn.

F G-L
tr. C. M.

Chapter Three

**The American Friend/Eden Mills, VT**

At twenty years of age, Philip H. Cummings was both a man of the world and the prodigal son. Born in Hardwick, Vermont in 1906, he had decided to do the world travelling usually reserved for the post-University years in his late teens and twenties. In 1928 he found himself in Spain, at Madrid's Residencia. Not engaged in any formal studies program, he had met Federico Garcia-Lorca after hearing him play piano in one of the school's common rooms. Like many before and after, he was taken by the poet's magnetism, even if he couldn't understand English. Cummings had enough Spanish for the two of them to become friends.

After losing track of Garcia-Lorca during his emotional and spiritual crisis, the two met up again as Cummings was to continue his travels and Garcia-Lorca was decamping to New York City. The embarkation point was England, and the two rode that far together. Cummings tendered his invitation for Garcia-Lorca to head north from the city to visit him at his family's summer camp in Eden Mills, Vermont.

All New Yorkers leave town in the summer months if they can, and to say that Garcia-Lorca was ready for the country after spending June into August in the city heat is an understatement. He contacted his new friend to say he would be on his way, if only for ten days. He would then visit Angel del Rio in the rustic town of Shandaken, in New York State, before returning to his studies, almost all of which were now outside the classroom.

He was excited and somewhat frightened by the poetry he had written since his arrival in New York. He may still have been depressed by things in Spain, but he was spared the creative sterility in this modern Inferno that had been part of his crisis back home. He was out of poetic stasis, poked and prodded by the stimulation of the foreign city's vast panorama and multiculturalism.

What stimulus would a fortnight in the country provide him, this Poet so in love with the Spanish earth of his youth and young manhood, which nourished him and his poetry and plays? His Imagination applied to Nature in her most minute detail produced a synesthesia that was a far cry from the dark heat of the urban imagery he had given himself over to since coming to America. With a little help from his friends deciphering a train schedule and getting aboard at the station, practical matters at which Garcia-Lorca was entirely inept, it was compass North to storm Eden.

His Host could not have been more delighted to see the man he now hero-worshipped arrive in Middlebury, VT for a nighttime ride to Lake Eden. "You have taken me out of the dungeon," Garcia-Lorca told him on the platform. It must have been a cleansing of the senses to fall asleep in total darkness punctuated only by the sounds from the woods and lakeside. His host introduced him to the other members of his family and the home cooking and baking was like manna to the Poet.

They began hiking around the lake, Garcia-Lorca no doubt a few paces off that of Cummings. If he had been in danger of looking like a rube in the city, up country he looked like a dude in his V-necked sweater, shirt and tie, pressed trousers and cordovan loafers. Even so, he was a celebrity, and Cummings acquainted him with the rest of his friends and introduced him to the local eccentrics, native Vermonters unimpressed by anyone "from away."

The change from concrete to pine needles beneath his feet and the temperature drop by the lakeside was welcome, though it made Garcia-Lorca more homesick for Spain than had his place in the urban labyrinth. Cummings recalled that on one of their hikes, the Poet had become enthused to build alters with the stones, ferns and flowers they found, only to pull them apart as an artificiality that could never compete with the natural order in the forest primeval. Balanchine said, "Man assembles; God creates." Though it had never been his style to hold a mirror up to Nature in his writing, it seems as if he didn't need any reminders that his persona itself was considered Against Nature. (Unless your nature was homosexual.) His poetry had lenses that took a microscopic view of things, then exfoliated out in his imagination into imagery so encoded and hermetic that at times it seems only three Bronze Goddesses, an Enigma machine and the Easter Table could solve it. This is not as much of a problem for the modern reader, with access to his collected works in order of their appearance.

The two had already set up their fair weather writing workshop on the cabin porch, and in this bucolic setting the Poet picked up his writing again. Outwardly, this setting might have been the Paradise of his Divine Comedy, but it would prove instead to be its Purgatory, given the poems Garcia-Lorca was putting out, pages falling to the floor like the leaves from the trees in an early intimation of autumn. Cummings wrote verse, and the Poet put him to the make-work task of translating his favorite book, "SONGS." That he did not give him "Gypsy Ballads," his most popular volume to date, shows that he wanted to distance himself from the "Gypsy Poet," image, and that Bunuel and Dali's criticism still stung. Despite the best seller status of the "Gypsy Ballads," "SONGS," is the better book.

For his part, Cummings took his friend at his word, that he wanted a book of his poetry translated into English. Not knowing Garcia-Lorca's aversion to the actual process of delivering a finished manuscript for publication, the young man could barely contain his natural ambitions. How many of the poems were translated with Master at the elbow of his Acolyte is not known, and would be a point of contention in the decades to come.

Cummings knew this was his brush with greatness, and he intended to make the most of it. Garcia-Lorca had learned virtually no English, so he could only count on Cummings fluency in Spanish to capture the nuances of his particular idiom, a task seasoned academics would fail at in the future. Again, Garcia-Lorca was a poet; Cummings wrote verse. The difference is as considerable as their language barrier and the ten years between them.

As things turned out, Cummings did some of his most creative writing and lecturing on his relationship and collaboration with the Poet. I'm sure he did not anticipate outliving him by many decades, and that he was truly grieved by the untimely event of his death. He referred to their time at Lake Eden, and his later visits to him in Spain, as the happiest days of his life. Later he claimed that he and Garcia-Lorca had been lovers since their first meeting at the Residencia in Madrid. He soon realized that without Garcia-Lorca there to refute or contradict him, there were many stories he might tell, or embellish as the years passed. In the meantime, publishers passed on his translation of "SONGS": "Assisted by Federico Garcia-Lorca. "

Between Garcia-Lorca's imaginative retelling of the genesis of his poetry and chronology of events in his life, one still must ask why, if he and Cummings were so close, he didn't do more to get the translation of "SONGS" in to print, especially when Cummings visited him again in Spain after his Vermont stay in 1929. Perhaps one of Garcia-Lorca's literary friends or former mentors told him that the assisted translation was serviceable, at best, making him want a better English version of his collection to make his debut.

Back at Lake Eden, things were already beginning to pall for Garcia-Lorca, like the fog that rolled in after a couple days of rain and confined them to quarters. He wrote to a friend that he was beginning to find his companion's attention cloying, something of an irony, considering half the reason he had come to America was his paramour tiring of HIS constancy. The Lover, and the One who is Loved, an old song the Poet should have been able to apply to his own scenario, to tragi-comic effect. In the same letter mentioned above, he described his days as working from morning to dusk and, after wishing there was a real drink in the house, turning in early to repeat the process the next day.

He was already starting to look forward to visiting his friend, Angel del Rio, in rural New York State. This restlessness was symptomatic of the depression his was still struggling with, and the fatigue of putting up a façade for his hosts. If he courted the duende, he was also afraid of it, being Death's familiar. Only his continued poetic output kept disaster at bay. Despite his place as honored guest in a place of great natural beauty, his poems were starting to read like variations on a suicide note. It also seems doubtful that if he was in a romance with his younger friend, he would have been quite so anxious to move on.

This is another interval in Garcia-Lorca's life when one wishes for the clarity of an impartial observer, but it seems that is exactly the kind of person who was scarce in the life of the Poet. His close friends were protective of him, or had a relationship with him they wished to keep private. There was a measure of discretion in these matters then, that no matter how curious the reader may be, he can only lament as a loss of manners in our age of social media and surveillance. His family received their son's bold front traveler's correspondence, which they had no reason to question, and most others kept their own counsel. Biography's loss was poetry's gain, and Garcia-Lorca lived the Life and paid the price.

SEAN ANDREW HEANEY

IV
POEMS OF LAKE EDEN MILLS
To Eduardo Ugarte

**Double Poem of Lake Eden**

> *Our cattle graze, the wind sends forth its breath.*
> -Garcilaso

It was the voice I had before,
ignorant of the dense and bitter sap,
the one that came lapping at my feet
beneath the moist and fragile ferns.

*Ay,* my love's voice from before
*ay,* voice of my truth,
*ay,* voice of my open side,
when all the roses spilled from my tongue
and the grass hadn't felt the horses impassable teeth!

Here you are drinking my blood,
drinking the humor of the heavy child I was,
while my eyes are shattered by aluminum
and drunken voices in the wind.

Let me pass through the arch
where Eve devours ants
and Adam impregnates the dazzling fish.
Little men with horns, let me return
to the grove of easy living
and the somersaults of pure joy.

I know the most secret way
to use an old rusty pin,
and I know the horror of eyes wide-awake
on the concrete surface of a plate.

But I want neither world nor dream, divine voice,
I want my liberty, my human love
in the darkest corner of the breeze no one wants.

My human love!

Those sea-dogs chase each other
and the wind lies in ambush for careless tree trunks,
Oh, voice of before, let your tongue burn
this voice of tin and talc!

I want to cry because I feel like it-
the way children cry in the last row of seats-
because I'm not a man, not a poet, not a leaf,
only a wounded pulse that probes the things of the other side.

I want to cry saying my name,
rose, child, and fir on the shore of this lake,
to speak truly as a man of blood
killing in myself the mockery and suggestive power of the word.

No, no, I'm not asking, I desire,
my liberated voice lapping at my hands.
In the labyrinth of folding screens my nakedness receives
the punishing moon and the clock covered with ash.

I was speaking that way.
I was speaking that way when Saturn stopped the trains
and the fog and the Dream and Death were looking for me.
Looking for me
where cattle with the little feet of a page bellow
and my body floats between contrary equilibriums.

SEAN ANDREW HEANEY

**Living Sky**

I won't be able to complain
though I never found what I was looking for.
Near the dried-up stones and the husks of insects,
I won't see the sun's duel with the creatures of flesh and blood.

But I'll go to the first landscape
of shocks, fluids, and murmurs
that seeps into a newborn child,
and where all surfaces are avoided,
so I'll know that my search has a joyful target
when I'm flying, jumbled with love and sands.

There, the frost of snuffed-out eyes won't reach,
nor the bellowing of a tree, murdered by the caterpillar.
There, all the shapes intertwine and have
the same frenetic, forward expression.

You can't pass through the swarming corollas—
the air dissolves your teeth of sugar.
And you can't caress the elusive fern
without feeling the utter astonishment of ivory.

There, under roots and in the marrow of the air,
you can grasp the truth of mistaken things.
The finest wave about to pounce on the chrome swimmer
and the flock of nocturnal cattle with a woman's little red feet...

I won't be able to complain
though I never found what I was looking for,
but I'll go to the first humid landscape of heartbeats
so I'll know that my search has a joyful target
when I'm flying, jumbled with love and sands.

I'm used to the cool air when I fly over empty beds.
Over squalls and ships run aground.
I stumbled sleepily through eternity's fixed hardness
and love at last without dawn. Love. Visible love!

*Eden Mills, Vermont. August 24, 1929*

VI
INTRODUCTION TO DEATH
*(Poems of Solitude in Vermont)*          *For Rafael Sanchez Ventura*

**Death**          *To Isidoro de Blas*

How hard they try!
How hard the horse tries
to become a dog.
How hard the dog tries to become a swallow.
How hard the swallow tries to become a bee.
How hard the bee tries to become a horse.
And the horse,
what a sharp arrow it squeezes from the rose,
what an ashen rose rising from its lips!
And the rose,
what a flock of lights and cries
knotted in the living sugar of its trunk.
And the sugar,
what daggers it dreams in its vigils!
And these miniature daggers,
what a moon without stables, what naked flesh,
what undying and rosy skin they seek out!
And I, on the roof's edge,
what a burning angel I look for and am.
But the plaster arch,
how vast, how invisible, how minute,
without even trying!

SEAN ANDREW HEANEY

**Nocturne of Emptied Space**

I

*If you want to see that nothing is left,*
*see the emptied spaces and the clothes,*
*give me your lunar glove,*
*you other glove of grass,*
*my love!*

The air can tear dead snails
from the elephant's lung
and blow the stiff, cold worms
from budding light or apples.

Faces erased of all emotion sail
beneath the faint uproar of the grass
and the frog's little breast is in the corner
with a clouded heart and mandolin.

On the great deserted plaza,
the cow's freshly severed head kept bellowing
and shapes that looked for the serpent's coiling
crystallized completely.

*If you want to see that nothing is left,*
*give me your speechless, emptied space, my love,*
*nostalgia for the academy and sad sky!*
*If you want to see that nothing is left!*

Inside you, my love, in your flesh,
the silence of derailed trains!
So many mummies' arms in bloom!
What a dead-end sky, my love, what a sky!

Stone in water, voice on the breeze-
love's limits burst free from their bleeding trunk.
Feeling the pulse of our love today is enough
to make flowers spring from other children.

*If you want to see that nothing is left,*
*see the emptied spaces of clouds and rivers,*
*give me your laurel boughs, my love.*
*If you want to see that nothing is left!*

The pure spaces spin through me, through you, at dawn,
preserving the tracks of the bloody branches
and some profile of tranquil plaster that depicts
the sudden pain of the moon, finished off with the dagger.

Look at the concrete shapes in search of their void.
Mistaken dogs and half-eaten apples.
Look at this sad fossil world, with its anxiety and anguish,
a world that can't find the accent of its very first sob.

When I search the bed for murmuring thread,
I know you've come, my love, to cover my roof.
The emptied space of an ant can fill the air,
but you moan with nothing to guide you through my eyes.

No, not through my eyes, because now you show me
four rivers wrapped tightly around your arm,
in the rough lean-to where the imprisoned moon
devours a sailor in front of the children.

*If you want to see that nothing is left,*
*my impenetrable love, now that you have gone,*
*don't give me your emptied space. No.*
*Mine is already traveling through the air!*

*Who will pity you, or me, or the breeze?*
*If you want to see that nothing is left.*

II

Me.
With the white emptied space of a horse,
ashen-maned. Pure and folded plaza,

Me.
My emptied space pierced with what remains of my armpits.
Like a neutered grapes shriveled skin and asbestos of dawn.

*All the world's light fits inside an eye.*
*The rooster crows and his song lasts longer then his wings.*

Me.
With the white emptied space of a horse.
Ringed by onlookers with their ant-teeming words.

In the circus of cold weather with no mutilated profile.
Among the chipped capitals of cheeks bled white.

Me.
My emptied space without you, city, without your voracious dead.
Rider through my life finally at the anchor.

Me.

*No new age. No enlightenment.*
*Only a blue horse and dawn.*

**Landscape with Two Graves and an Assyrian Dog**

Friend,
get up and listen
to the Assyrian dog howl.
Cancer's three nymphs have been dancing,
my son.
They carried mountains of red sealing wax
and stiff bed sheets to the place where cancer slept.
The horse had an eye in its neck
and the moon was in a sky so cold
that she had to tear open her mound of Venus
and drown the ancient graveyards in blood and ashes.

Friend,
wake up, the mountains still aren't breathing
and the grass of my heart is somewhere else.
It doesn't matter if you're full of seawater.
For a long time I have loved a child
who had a tiny feather on his tongue,
and we lived inside a knife for a hundred years.
Wake up. Be still. Listen. Sit up in your bed.
The howling
is a long purple tongue that releases
terrifying ants and the liquor of irises.
Here it comes toward the rock. Don't spread out your roots!
It approaches. Moans. Friend, don't sob in your dreams.

Friend!
Get up and listen
To the Assyrian dog howl.

SEAN ANDREW HEANEY

**Ruin**

*To Regina Sanz de la Maza*

Never finding itself,
traveling through its own white torso,
the air made its way!

Soon it was clear that the moon
Was a horse's skull,
and the air, a dark apple.

Behind the window,
with whips and lights, I felt
sand struggling with water.

I saw all the blades of grass arrive
and I threw a bleating lamb
to their little teeth and lancets.

The first dove, encased
in feathers and plastic,
flew inside a single drop.

Here comes the grass, son.
Its spit-swords ring
through the empty sky.

Hold my hand, my love. The grass!
Through the house's broken windows,
the blood unleashed its waves of hair.

Only you and I are left.
Prepare your skeleton for the air.
We're the only ones who remain.

Prepare your skeleton.
Hurry, love, hurry, we've got to look
for our sleepless profile.

**Two Lovers Murdered by a Partridge**

"They both wanted it," his mother told me. 'Both of them."

"My dear woman," I said, "that's impossible. You're too emotional, and at your age you should know why the dewdrops settle on the ground like pins."

"Be quiet, Luciano, be quiet. No, no, Luciano, no"

"In order to make the name bearable, I need to restrain my painful memories. And you think that I could be consoled for my sadness by that tiny set of teeth, and that child's hand, forgotten inside the wave?"

"They both wanted it," his cousin told me. "Both of them."

I contemplated the sea and suddenly I understood everything.

"Could it be that the moonlit pallor of that departing ocean liner comes from the beak of that cruel dove with an elephant's heart?"

"I remember I had to use my spoon several times to ward off the wolves. I wasn't to blame for anything. You know that. My God, I'm crying!"

"They both wanted it," I said. "Both of them. An apple will always be a lover, but a lover can't ever be an apple."

"That's why they died. That's why. At the age of twenty rivers and a single shredded winter."

"It was very simple. They made love above and beyond the museums."
Right hand
with left hand.
Left hand
with right hand.
Right foot
with right foot.
Left foot
with cloud
Hair
with sole of the foot.
Sole of the foot
with left cheek.

Oh, left cheek! Oh, northwest of little boats and ants of mercury! Give me the handkerchief, Genoveva; I'm going to cry... I'm going to cry until a bunch of immortelles emerges from my eyes...They were going to bed.

There was no other spectacle so tender...
Did you hear me?

They were going to bed!
Left thigh
with left forearm.
Closed eyes
with open fingernails.
Waist with nape,
and with shoreline.
And the four little ears were four angels in a snowy cabin. They yearned for each other. They made love. Defying the law of gravity. The difference between a rose thorn and a Star is very simple.
When they figured this out, they left for the countryside.
They made love.
My god! They made love while the chemists watched.
Their backs with the earth,
earth with anise.
Moon with a sleeping shoulder.
And their waists entwined, whispering like glass.
I saw their cheeks tremble when the professors brought them honey and vinegar in a tiny sponge. Many times they had to scare away the dogs that howled in the pure white ivy of the bed. But they made love.
They were man and woman,
in other words,
a man
and a little piece of earth,
an elephant
and a child,
a child and a bulrush.
They were two young men who had fainted
and a chrome plated leg.
They were boatmen!
Yes.
They were the terrible boatmen of the Guadiana, who crush all the world's roses with their oars.
The old sailor spit tobacco from his mouth, and yelled to frighten away the gulls. But it was too late.
When the women in mourning arrived at the governor's mansion, he was quietly eating green almonds and cold fish from an exquisite gold plate. It would have been better not to have spoken with him.
In the Azores.

I'm nearly unable to cry.
I sent two telegrams, but unfortunately it was too late.
Very late.
I can only tell you that the two children, passing by the edge of the forest, saw a partridge that trailed a little thread of blood from its beak.
That's the reason, my dear captain, for my strange melancholia.

**Moon and Panorama of the Insects**
*(Love Poem)*

> *"The moon shimmers on the sea,*
> *the wind moans on the sail*
> *and raises gently swelling*
> *blue and silver waves."*
> *-ESPRONCEDA*

My heart would take the shape of a shoe
if a siren lived in every village.
But the night never ends when it leans on the sick,
and there are ships that want to be seen in order to sink in peace.

If the wind blows softly,
my heart takes the shape of a girl.
If the wind won't leave the cane fields,
My heart takes the shape of a millenary cow pie.

Row, row, row, row,
toward the army of jagged points,
toward a landscape of pulverized ambushes.
Equal night of the snow, the discontinued systems.
And the moon.
The moon!
But not the moon.
The taverns' vixen.
The Japanese rooster that ate its own eyes.
The cud.

The tapeworms behind glass won't save us,
nor herbariums where the metaphysician
meets the other slopes of the sky.
Shapes are a lie. What is there?
The circle of mouths of the oxygen
And the moon.
But not the moon.
The insects,
little dead things lining the shores,
sorrow on longitude,

iodine on stitched flesh,
the crowd on the head of a pin,
the naked man who kneads everyone's blood,
and my love who is neither horse nor burn,
creature whose breast was consumed.
My love!

Now they sing, scream, moan: *A face. Your face! A face.*
*The apples are one,*
*the dahlias identical,*
*the light tastes like worn-out metal*
*and the countryside of half a decade will fit on the cheek of a coin.*
*But your face covers the skies of the feast.*
Now they sing, scream, moan,
cover everything, climb, terrify!

We've got to move- Hurry up!- through the waves, the branches,
the deserted streets of the Middle Ages going down to the river,
the stores of hides where a wounded cow's horn bellows,
up the ladders- Don't be scared!- up the ladders.
A discolored man is bathing in the sea;
he's so tender that the searchlights ate him as he gambled away his heart,
and a thousand women live in Peru- Oh, insects!- night and day
they weave nocturnes and parades among their own veins.

One tiny corrosive glove stops me. That's enough!
I feel the crackle of the first
broken vein on my handkerchief.
Watch out for your hands and feet, my love,
since I must give up my face,
my face, my face, yes, my half-eaten face!

This chaste, burning desire of mine,
this confusion from longing for equilibrium,
this innocent sorrow of gunpowder in my eyes,
will lighten the anguish of another heart
consumed by the nebulae.

The people in shoe stores won't save us,
nor the landscapes becoming music when they find the rusted keys.

## SEAN ANDREW HEANEY

Breezes are a lie. Only a small cradle
exists, in the attic,
that remembers everything.
And the moon.
But not the moon.
The insects.
Just the insects,
crackling, biting, quivering, swarming,
and the moon
with a glove of smoke in the doorway of its wreckage.
The moon!!!

*New York, January 4, 1930*

Chapter Four

**Notes on The Poems**

Garcia-Lorca had to wait to reach his pastoral idyll in "Double Poem of Lake Eden" to have his Dark Night of the Soul. That appellation comes from the writings of his fellow countryman and poet, St. John of the Cross. For the religious, it represents the absence of God, which results in a negation of the self and the spirit. The natural and spiritual world seem dead and the imagination sterile.

The saint-to-be must rely on Faith in what cannot be apprehended by the soul or the senses. The poet is not vouchsafed the comfort that the Faith will return after this great trial of body and spirit. While certain verses of Garcia-Lorca's cri de coeur sound more like the temper tantrum of a spoiled child than the fear and trembling and sickness unto Death undergone by the acolyte, it is still shocking at this midway point in the poet's journey.

After directing his voice and vision to the seeming fallen world of the urban landscape and its denizens, now he confronts his own image, as if reflected in the lake-as-mirror, only to see the self spilt down the middle, "where my body floats between contrary equilibriums." None of St. Sebastian's negative capability in being rent physically and emotionally here. He invokes the spirit of St. Lucy, patron saint of writers, who, being sold into marriage rather than realizing her dream of the convent, gouges out her eyes, which God then restores to her before her ultimate demise. Garcia-Lorca writes about the oedipal act like a backstreet abortion. "I know the most secret way/to use an old rusty pin,/and I know the horror of eyes wide-awake/on the concrete surface of a plate."

Before evoking idealized childhood visions versus suicidal darkness, he hopes for an easeful Death passing "through the arch where Eve devours ants and Adam impregnates the dazzling fish." But this is not to be his lot, the only way out is through, so he makes his demands to the universe: "I want my liberty, my human love/in the darkest corner of the breeze no one wants. My human love!"

Life, disprized love and the burden of his visions put him beside himself: "I want to cry because I feel like it---Because I'm not a man, not a poet, not a leaf/only a wounded pulse that probes the things of the other side. . .I want to cry saying my name,/rose, child, and fir on the shore of this lake."

In the first draft of this poem, the poet had written; "I want to cry speaking my name,/ Federico Garcia-Lorca, on the shore of this lake;/ to speak truly as a man of blood/killing in myself the mockery and the suggestive power of the word." Self abnegation and the renouncing of his vocation, it is a suicide in all but the act. It is that pulling back, the hesitation to use his real name that puts the poem back on the artistic plane and the poet not ready to resign himself to oblivion, whether through a glimmer of Faith or through the reconciliation of the "two lonely halves," of his persona to salvage the title of poet and save himself from his selves.

There are some fairly self-deprecating and nihilistic poems in the remainder of the pastoral sequence, but never again will Garcia-Lorca resign the distance of the poet or the artifice of his Art; no matter how obsessed with death the remaining poems may be, even announced in their title, it is still Death in the abstract, with the poet using all the style and craft at his command to navigate his way from this pivotal point of no return; back on track in his journey of Life.

Already in "Living Sky," Garcia-Lorca seems reconciled with the return to the eternal struggle of Eros and Death: "I won't be able to complain/though I never found what I was looking for." The title may refer to an evening of the appearance of the Northern Lights over Lake Eden with Mount Norris as a fixed black backdrop. But that is from the gospel according to his ever eager companion, Philip Cummings, and not related until many years later, when such melodramatic episodes from his memory were being questioned for their veracity.

The title does seem to refer to Garcia-Lorca taking flight to continue his search for, "visible Love!" Not unlike his then unpublished and never finished scenario for a silent film, "Trip To the Moon," (now in The Complete Poems,") the telluric and the cosmic seem to intertwine. ". . .I'll go to the first landscape of shocks, fluids, and murmurs/that seeps into a newborn child,/ and where all surfaces are avoided,/so I'll know that my search has a joyful target/when I'm flying, jumbled with love and sands." And repeats: "I won't be able to complain/though I never found what I was looking for;/but I'll go to the first humid landscape of heartbeats/so I'll know that my search has a joyful target/when I'm flying,/jumbled with love and sands. . . I stumble sleepily through eternity's fixed hardness/and love at last without dawn."

In the final draft of the book, the remaining poems from Vermont are interrupted by the three poems Garcia-Lorca wrote staying with his friend, Angel del Rio, in the New York State countryside. Two poems, grimmer than Grimm's fairytales, (which the poet had studied,) concern a young boy and girl the poet met among the farms and homesteads where his friend had summer lodgings. They are separated by a savage poem of bovine slaughter that again makes the reader shudder at the poet's state of mind. It is not a relief to know that the aspects of death and disease that shadow the two children's stories are products of Garcia-Lorca's imagination. For a poet who idealized his own childhood as a Golden Age, the reader might think that the kind of fatality and creeping sickness in these poems might be better left to the urban world he so obviously despised. But like the poems of Lake Eden, these poems show that for the poet there is no rural respite for death hard at work every moment beneath the surface of the landscapes or their inhabitants.

After the rustic horror show of the New York State poems, one can almost laugh at the title of the section of the rural Purgatorial realm: INTRODUCTION TO DEATH (Poems of Solitude in Vermont.) The poems are not without black comedy, parody, pastiche, and genuine beauty. This, Part VI in, "Poet of New York," is a tour-de-force of style and deliberate play on the obsessive imagery from what has come before it.

"Death" is a children's song about dreamed incongruities in the natural order of things, an insectary and bestiary of a child's garden who can't relate to the irrefutability of the natural cycle for plants, insects and beasts; even the Human animal. It moves from the imaginative child's incomprehension that he himself is a part of this cycle, and that "Nature is not made in the image of man's compassion," to the "mature" poet's image of himself as a burning angel on the roof's edge, watching all of earthly life passing through the blinding white archway of death, echoed from the Lake Eden poems. Outside the Natural order and biological imperatives, an apostate to salvation through Faith, all things pass away and only Death is certain.

"Nocturne of Emptied Space," is perhaps the most beautiful of the poems in the cycle, along with "Moon and Panorama of the Insects (Love Poem.)" This song of Dark Love finds the poet lamenting lost love of people places and things, though in an almost Zen like way, things absent are still represented by their void, or negative image. He seems to be speaking from the other side, represented by the "white void" of a horse. It concludes with a vision of end times, in the place of any rebirth or salvation: "No new age. No enlightenment./Only a blue horse and dawn." Eternity after Humanity.

"Landscape with Two graves and an Assyrian Dog," continues in the afterlife of two dead men awakened in the cemetery by the howling of an Assyrian dog. Assyrian Christians are one of earliest communities of disciples of Christ. Perhaps this poem is a response to Garcia-Lorca being cast as the Andalusian Dog in the film by Bunuel and Dali. In this poem, an erotically charged, "Waiting for Godot," the promised resurrection of the Catholic Church abandoned by all of the triumvirate, is only a lone dog's night time howl that has the two friends able only to reckon up their sexual fulfillment in life.

"Ruin," harkens back to the "joyful target," of "Living Sky." "Never finding itself,/traveling through its own white torso,/the air made its way!" This is a poem of realizing one's self alone and with another, a flowering of love in a ruined landscape in the face of a rapidly approaching Death that will spare nothing but insects and an implacable moon: "Soon it was clear that the moon/was a horse's skull,/and the air, a dark apple." Again the symbol of an inverse Genesis, with love sacramentalized in place of the deliverance from death through Christ's sacrifice.

After the urgency of the lover/unbeliever's liturgy of the past two poems, Garcia-Lorca insures that these poems and the two that follow are a literary tour-de-force, as well as a heretic's gospels. "Two Lovers Murdered by a Partridge," is surreal satire of a drawing room farce, divided by a sailor's ballad. The subject is two dead bodies found still entwined in a love embrace and the reactions of a stock cast of characters and God in the persona of an old ship's Captain. The two lovers might also be a double suicide, and that, as well as them both being men, seems to be the fate that the others must learn to understand and to live with. Garcia-Lorca's sense of humor hasn't been on display in the majority of the poems that would become, "Poet in New York," but this poem is a prime example of it.

"Moon and Panorama of the Insects (Love Poem,)" concludes the Introduction to Death/Poems of Solitude in Vermont, and it is a grand finale in the way it pulls together all the threads of the poems in the cycle. There is a touch of the mordant humor of Garcia-Lorca in the subtitle, (Love Poem,) and the poet plays on this throughout what is the final flow chart of this world and it's relentless metamorphosis distorted in the life and mind, time and space continuum of a human life span. For all its pain and suffering, the poet endows this world with his love, especially if he sees no solace or life after this one:

> "This chaste, burning desire of mine,/this confusion from longing for equilibrium,/this innocent sorrow of gunpowder in my eyes,/will lighten the anguish of another heart/consumed by the nebulae."

While this verse seems to promise some peace to the divided self of Garcia-Lorca, and redeem his human love as worth living and dying for, the last stanza mitigates that promise by the poet succumbing to a teeming river of insects under the Death's headstone of the moon.

The provincial poet who had vented his spleen on the cityscape of Gotham, fled to the country only to find that he met the enemy, himself and his demons and angels, waiting for him. After denouncing himself in the bitterest terms, finding himself at the bottom of his personality looking up, he has to make peace through the gift of recounting his vision in words. If Garcia-Lorca "never found what he was looking for," in this Eden, he could console himself in the knowledge that he had escaped from poetic stasis. Thus fortified, and fulfilled in the only way possible for him in his vocation, he escaped the mist and chill of Vermont's early Autumn. Boarding his train, he told his friend Philip Cummings, "You'll bury me in this fog," as he returned to the city and the next calamity. He had not seen the last of his American friend.

Chapter Five

**The Depression & Paradise Regained**

Since his arrival in New York, Garcia-Lorca and the rest of the country had been living on the last bubble of the Jazz Age, or the roaring twenties. What happened next would make the poet with his Jeremiads against the modern metropolis seem like a prophet.

In October of 1929, on what would henceforth be called, Black Tuesday, the stock market crashed. The bonds of fortune became so much play money, not worth the paper it was printed on. A panic ensued, as brokers and stockholders desperately tried to save the paper tiger. Garcia-Lorca claimed he went out and stood in the middle of this stream of humanity flooding Wall Street, dodging the falling stockholders, taking it in with a grim satisfaction. There were many stories of suicides by those who had gone from prince to pauper, but there was only one dry dive recorded in the Times; ironically, a man from Vermont.

Garcia-Lorca returned to his friends in the Spanish community, frustrating those who tried and tried again to teach him English and satisfying himself with work on the poems that would make up, "Poet In New York." He also completed a play within a play, "The Public," a meditation on the theater that for many years was considered a lost work. When finally presented, it proved to be the most modern and abstract of all his plays, ahead of it's time in technique, but familiar in it's themes of homosexual love expressed in the masks and make up of the stage and backstage, in character and out of character.

It was the prospect of his departure after the New Year to Cuba, and then back to Spain, that sustained the poet as much as his creativity. He continued his blistering broadsides against the City, the Catholic Church and the inequalities in the diversity of its people, as only a man of means and an apostate from his Faith can write them. He still took communion at Midnight Mass on Christmas at St. Paul's Cathedral, which he wrote home about, calling the church the most beautiful he had ever seen, in New York or in Spain.

In March he would be writing them from Cuba, a Paradiso where the poor might go barefoot, but at least they smile through it and speak his language. He was celebrated in the upper classes and the literary and academic circles. He gave lectures and readings, and was regarded as a native son before the return voyage to Spain. He would never visit North America again, and would never have predicted that future events in and out of Spain would see his entire family and many friends immigrate there, not long after he reached the height of fame, and notoriety, in South America and in his native land.

Chapter Six

**Last Act/Last August**

The prodigal returned to his family in Granada and his friends at the Residencia in Madrid. Garcia-Lorca was still in the full flush of his writings from abroad. He did not know just how far ahead of the curve his poems and unfinished play had put him from his audience of friends, rivals and colleagues. The free verse screeds of his poetry had pushed surrealism past the understanding of the majority, and even those who should have been most sympathetic to his abstract play, "The Public," made the title sound even more ironic than had been intended.

If he cared much about the cool or uncomprehending reception, he didn't let on. He was about to embark on the three rural tragedies that would make his name as a playwright; "Blood Wedding," "Yerma," and "The House of Bernarda Alba." This trilogy would make him famous in his lifetime, though he would never see the last of these reach the stage. His two modern plays, "The Public," and "When Five Years Pass," would also be posthumous productions.

Garcia-Lorca loved seeing his characters and the world he created for them come to life in the same way that he hated seeing his collections of poetry "dead on the page." Certainly none of his poetry readings had been greeted with the enthusiasm of his plays. Called by a friend a connoisseur of feminine psychology, his powerful roles for women had the best actresses in Spain and South America anxious to play them, and their success put the author in the limelight. Unfortunately, this made him more visible to his detractors and censors as well. He would go on to produce classic Spanish plays, and his own, to more acclaim. He even built a company of his own to perform those plays all over Spain, in some cases to people who had never been to the theater in their lives. The Poet, who had declared himself on the side of those who have nothing, was especially satisfied with the productions of his roving band of players to the masses. He was still writing poetry, but his plays had taken pride of place.

The intoxication of being the man of letters in their midst, prompted Garcia-Lorca to speak rather too freely to the popular press, now wanting to know his views on matters literary as well as politics. He continued to talk about helping the poor, and speaking out against the government and the Church. Off the record, supposedly, he even spelled out the nature of his homosexuality: "The fact of the matter, if what you say is true, is that you are as abnormal as I am. Because in fact I am. Because I have only known men; and you know that the homosexual, the fairy makes me laugh, amuses me with his womanish itch to wash, iron and sew, to paint himself, to wear skirts, to speak with effeminate faces and gestures. But I don't like it. Normality is neither your way of only women, or mine. What's normal is love without limits. Because love is more and better than the morality of a dogma, Catholic morality; there is no one can make me resign myself to the sole stance of having children. In my way there is no misrepresentation. Both are as they are. Without switching. There is no one who gives orders; there is no one who dominates; there is no submission. There is no assigning of roles. There is no substitution or imitation There is only abandon and joyous mutual possession. But it would take a real revolution. A new morality, a morality of complete freedom. That is what Walt Whitman was asking for. And that may be the freedom the New World will proclaim: the heterosexualism in which America lives. Just like the ancient world."

Again, this was a subject written off the record, not published until many years later. But a by-product of fame was the idea that he was immune to the forces who would hold speaking freely against him. Never circumspect in his life or his writing, his enemies had no trouble building a case against him, for his seeming Socialist stance or in the demi-monde of his sex life. In the latter, he was a true revolutionary, but the Civil War about to rend his country in two would not be the bloodless revolution of enlightened views on sexuality and a new deal for the poor. Spain was choosing sides, and real world events were about to overcome Federico Garcia-Lorca, even in his stature as his countries greatest writer.

Garcia-Lorca was a man of the people in that he had friends on the Communist and Fascist side, most of whom knew that the poet was apolitical. All were unanimous in trying to get him to leave the country. Bunuel, a Red sympathizer, would go into years of exile, and make his greatest films abroad. Dali was already an expatriate, who would do an about face later, shaving his head, converting to Catholicism and announcing that henceforth he would take the inspiration for his painting from the Old Masters. Cynical or obtuse, both of Garcia-Lorca's colleagues were more mature in their reading of Spain's future for the artist. Once betrayed to the fascists, he could only say, "I haven't done anything." Nothing to be murdered for, but thousands at the mercy of Communism or Fascism in the future would find that the validity of their plea made no difference if you were considered an enemy of the state, or "of the people," as the Socialist would have it.

The poet had his Eden; now he would have his Gethsemane. Taken to olive groves in a cul-de-sac, Garcia-Lorca and three fellow travelers were told what their fate was to be, then left for a couple hours to sweat it out. Garcia-Lorca was said to be so frightened that he had forgotten the prayers his mother had taught him. The stoppage of prayer, in the handbook of the Inquisition, meant that the person was in the presence of Evil, and in this case they got that right. The four were allegedly lined up and shot by a firing squad. It must have been their captors way of making this a correct military execution, but this usually reserved for soldiers, and since it was done in secret, and the bodies planted where they have yet to be recovered, it seems strange they would accord them this dubious honor, which even war criminals have to request as special treatment. To try to find logic or justice in such a farcical fatality is perhaps the biggest folly of all. Spain's greatest poet now belonged to the ages, and to the Spanish earth. An even greater cataclysm, the Second World War, followed hard upon the Fascist "victory" in the Spanish civil war. But that morning in August, 1936, was six years, almost to the day, from when "Saturn stopped the trains," and Garcia-Lorca spent more than a week but less than a fortnight in Eden. His testament of those days has outlived him, and helped make him a legend.

Chapter Seven

**The Unreliable Narrator & The Rogue Scholar**

Another refugee from Spain was Garcia-Lorca's Vermont host and friend, Philip Cummings. He had followed the Poet back to Spain, as acolyte and would be lover, while continuing to study at the Residencia. It was perhaps on this visit that he first pressed to have the "assisted" translation of Garcia-Lorca's, "SONGS," published. It is possible that he learned that the Poet was interested in the work he was writing in the present tense, or was to write, more than having his second book published in a translation of a language he had made a concerted effort not to master. If Cummings was rebuffed at this juncture, it wouldn't be the last time. He left Spain when the storm was gathering, and is thought to have seen Garcia-Lorca only once more, and briefly, in 1934. He returned to Vermont and received a degree at Middlebury College. He genuinely mourned the Poet's death in 1936.

After their son's execution, the Garcia-Lorca family immigrated to the United States at the first opportunity. The poet's brother, Francisco, would make his own pilgrimage to Vermont, and to Middlebury College, where he was the head of the summer Spanish program for nine years. Perhaps he and Cummings crossed paths, but the only known exchange between the two is when Francisco Garcia-Lorca refused Cummings permission to reprint the Spanish originals of the poems in "SONGS." Cummings finally found a publisher for his assisted translation in 1976, Duquesne University Press. He also petitioned a Spanish scholar, Daniel Eisenberg, to write an introduction and afterword to the volume. It must have seemed a golden opportunity for the Academic to be party to what he took to be the only translation of Federico Garcia-Lorca's poems assisted by the poet himself. He would also publish Cummings journal of the summer of '29, as well as two essays Cummings had written after Garcia-Lorca's death. The mid-Seventies was one of the many times since his death that readers and writers of poetry tried to promote interest in the life and works of the Poet. Many of his works were still unaccounted for, even after Franco had lifted the ban on his plays and poetry in Spain in the late fifties.

Philip Cummings had retired from a career as a lecturer, where he was much in demand, also from business and teaching. He had spent the fifties and sixties as the Gay-in-the gray flannel suit, even taking on the beard of a wife and two children. He took the frustrations of his double life out on them, becoming a heavy drinker in the process. He always felt that he had missed his calling as a poet for the security and respectability of the closeted life.

He had a few of his own verses printed in newspapers and literary journals. In 1944, he had a book of verse published by a small press, entitled; "Woodchuck Rampant Bearing Light," a title even Robert Frost wouldn't have been able to get away with. I was unable to find a copy, and the Cummings/Eisenberg "SONGS," in the tradition of "Small print, big words, no sales," has only one copy extant in the state of Vermont.

The critical reception was the sound of one hand clapping. Not bad enough to merit a thorough hatchet job, or good enough to win the author a place in the Garcia-Lorca canon, it maintains a spot in the half light as a literary curiosity. It did send scholars of Garcia-Lorca to visit Cummings, now widowed and alone, for his account of the poet and the work completed during his stay in Vermont. Those willing to listen heard increasingly embroidered fantasies of the relationship between the two men and the poetry and prose completed during that short stay.

Cummings relished the attention, after years of having been given the go by from Garcia-Lorca's family. They were in charge of the poet's work after his death, before there was a Lorca Foundation and the poet had achieved "World Class," status that he deserves and enjoys today. Cummings spoke of a voluminous auto- biographical document given to him by Garcia-Lorca, with strict orders to destroy said document in the event of his death. To hear him tell it, the contents were the Poet's settling scores, outing some of his lovers and companions and castigating the Catholic Church and meddlesome censorious authorities in Spain. While that doesn't sound out of the realm for Garcia-Lorca, the world will never know because Cummings allegedly burned it after reading it following the Poet's murder.

It was around this time that Cummings credibility began to be called in to question. Contrary versions of events started to come in to play, and Eisenberg, who had given the alleged assisted translation of "SONGS" credence and academic authority, had asked the Poet's family why they refused to have anything to do with the work; even its first run as a university press book had been retrograde to the family's wishes. Enough evidence against Cummings and his working relationship and personal recollections was passed on in the literary/academic circles to make him and his book poison.

The scholars and biographers stopped finding their way to Cummings door, and any future references in their work to Cummings and his "recollections," carried a caveat and asterisk. Alone now with his thoughts and dreams of Garcia-Lorca, growing old in all but his sexual desires, solitude bred corruption. After the teenage boys in the neighborhood began giving his house a wide berth after being importuned to do "odd jobs" for the old man, only children remained to be preyed upon. These transgressions and a diagnosis of creeping dementia landed the man who once spoke of knowing poets, celebrities and dining with kings, in a mental institution for the remainder of his days.

Eisenberg may have denounced Cummings in print and to the academic world, but rather than taking his cue from the latter's demise in 2002, he found himself driven to take on the Lorca Foundation and any of the Poet's friends, enemies or acquaintances who he felt were withholding letters, poems and plays from publication. He was going to take up the cudgel against censorship of these works in an outrageous posting: "Lorca and Censorship: The Gay Artist Made Heterosexual." RE the alleged censorship, he posted a 21 page tirade that didn't stop with that subject, but went on to what Eisenberg projected on to the unreleased or lost works of Garcia-Lorca. "I'm angry over it. It has made my life poorer. It offends my sense of how the world should be, of how writers and artists should be treated. It reflects the same spirit that killed Federico. How strange that the censorship of the Franco government, which was monolithic, has been much less problematical and influential than the selective censorship of Lorca's heirs."

He gets points for gall. He tips his hand to his own catapulting out of the closet in the briar patch that follows, projecting his own fantasies of what these censored works might contain, regardless of their literary merit in the Garcia-Lorca bibliography. For Eisenberg, in his speculation on why Garcia-Lorca's unpublished works would be censored, he wrote that Christ and his disciples were an early incarnation of the Mattachine Society, or a pioneering Gay coterie, with Jesus and John the Apostle as Bruce Wayne and useful ward, Dick Grayson. A work Garcia-Lorca mentioned before his death, "The Destruction of Sodom," would be an apologia against the taboos of pederasty and incest. Eisenberg should have shown more caution in his vile speculation on the latter work. Proust's chapter of almost the same title in, "Remembrance of Things Past," was an excoriation, however ironic in tone, of the homosexual characters in his magnum opus. Garcia-Lorca had done somewhat the same in his, "Ode To Walt Whitman," in "Poet In New York," lambasting openly gay behavior, mostly the swish and nelly, or overtly effeminate behavior up to and including the degeneracy of sexual abuse of children. Here he was again simpatico with the American poet, Hart Crane. Both he and Garcia-Lorca liked to make straight or sexually ambivalent men, of the rough and ready kind Whitman had written about. As Crane put it, "I never could stand too much falsetto, you know."

There is more paranoid ranting and self righteous rage in this moral screed available under the author's name, or its humorous title. He may have disdained swanning about, but the idea of Garcia-Lorca being made Heterosexual, is like trying to make Oscar Wilde into Charles Bukowski. The Lorca Foundation must have excommunicated Eisenberg with extreme prejudice to rate this hysterical blog. Even though he repudiates

Cummings again in his sanctimonious fashion in this document, what followed on-line about Professor Eisenberg renders the entire thing a moot point.

"Daniel B. Eisenberg, 64, of 91 Westchester Drive, Clifton Park, was sentenced March 16th, 2011, to one to one to 3 years in State prison, for the charge of failure to register as a sex offender. This sentencing is concurrent with a resentencing for violation of probation for the charge of possessing an obscene sexual performance by a child, a felony, for which Eisenberg was originally sentenced in 2003 to ten years probation." Saratoga Springs Police Department.

The last word on Eisenberg on-line was from one of his jaded colleagues at a Spanish Literature Conference a year later, when he opined that Professor Eisenberg was missed at this event, prompting another to comment: "He should have gotten life in prison for what he did."

As a guest of the state, Eisenberg is either having the time of his life or living in fear for it. Many time servers in American prisons were sexually abused as children and they will sometimes mete out justice to pedophiles themselves.

Garcia-Lorca liked young men, but not that young. As for being "for the poor," only poor children are more marginalized. The Poet would have been aghast at the child sex abuse scandal in our time which has shaken the Vatican to its foundation. He knew his gospel if the priesthood and bishops had forgotten it:

> "Truly I tell you, if you do not turn about and become as children are, you shall not enter the Kingdom of Heaven. He then who makes himself small as this child is, he shall be the greater in the Kingdom of Heaven. And if one accepts one child like this in my name, he accepts me. But if one leads astray one of these little ones who have faith in me, it is better for him to have a millstone hung about his neck and be drowned in the sea." Gospel of St. Matthew: 17.19-18.6

So we are left to behold the Man and the Artist, one who's works sound as contemporary as the day they were written, a man who Fate, or the Duende, put in the wrong place at the wrong time, an early casualty in the events of history in his home country. That he is one of the Immortals, there is no question. The publication of "Poet In New York," translated by Simon & White in 1988, was a high water mark that lifted all worthy crafts of others translations of his plays and poems. Many of the works once considered lost or censored, have since been published so that now, for the English reader, there is a bilingual Collected Poems of over 500 pages, and a Collected Plays weighing in at about half that.

The critical studies continue to be written, with two major biographies to date. What is most impressive and truly indicative of the far reaching popularity and respect for the Poet is the section of his bibliography titled, "List of Works Inspired by Lorca" that runs for six pages, listing poetry and novels, musical works, theater, films, and television.

Chapter Eight

**Garcia-Lorca, Martyr & Saint Innocent
Found in Translation**

Never in the fantasticon of his imagination would Garcia-Lorca have dreamt of the celebration that the 2nd revised and expanded edition of the Simon & White translation of Poet In New York, would receive in the city he vilified. The summer of 2013 in New York City was the fairest of the seasons for him and his epic poem. Among many varied events held from April to August was a panel discussion of the poetry he had written at Lake Eden, Vermont, and the events of two of "the summer people," in the Garden back in 1929. Lorca's art and the works it has inspired in every medium were performed and displayed at multiple venues throughout the city.

It can be decades before a translation of a foreign poet provides an understanding of the true stature of their work in their native tongue. The English translation of Russian poet Anna Akhmatova by D. M. Thomas, first printed in two separate volumes by Ohio State Press, now the representative collection of the master poet in the esteemed Penguin Poets series, is perhaps the best contemporary example.

Garcia-Lorca's "Poet In New York" would have to wait 48 years, until 1988, to find a trio of two translators and an editor to bring out an English language version of his epic poem more than worthy of the original Spanish. The Poet had already achieved worldwide fame for his plays and poems, and there had been many translations in many countries of both. He had reached the status of "World Class" Author posthumously years earlier, especially after censorship in Spain was relaxed following the long awaited death of its fossilized dictator, Generalissimo Franco.

The martyr's death his minions had given Garcia-Lorca in 1936 had immortalized him as more than a writer and artist. He was, and remains, an almost religious cultural icon, as a pioneering Gay writer, a Socialist crusader, a scholar and an exponent of the diversity of his country's past, while his poetry has stayed modern. It has influenced contemporary writers, musicians, painters, filmmakers and choreographers. For critics, literary historians and biographers, the Life, Work and Death of Federico Garcia-Lorca have become a cottage industry. Though many writers have been lionized this way, it is the mysteries and ellipses in the life, work, death, and afterlife of Garcia-Lorca that mark him out as a distinctive character. His work has survived a Civil War that he didn't, a Second World War, and a host of social, cultural and artistic changes and customs.

Now he is Everyman's poet and playwright. His life and works continue to inspire, and the reader can only speculate what he would have accomplished had he lived into old age. He effected those who knew him as a true poet and spirit of his time. With all that has been written about him, I will let Federico Garcia-Lorca have what he was denied in life, the last word:

>My heart of silk
>is filled with lights,
>with lost bells,
>with lilies and bees.
>I will go very far,
>farther than those hills,
>farther than the seas,
>close to the stars,
>to beg Christ the Lord
>to give back the soul I had
>of old, when I was a child,
>ripened with legends,
>with a feathered cap
>and a wooden sword.

\* \* \*

**Bibliography: Poetry & Plays by Federico Garcia-Lorca (1898-1936)**

Collected Poems: The Poetical Works – poems in English & Spanish. Multiple translators. Critical matter in English by Christopher Maurer, Farar, Straus & Giroux. New York. 1st Edition hc, 1991. New York, NY.

Selected Poems: edited by Francisco Garcia Lorca & Donald M. Allen. Multiple translators. Poems in English & Spanish. New Directions pb, 3rd Printing, 1961 New York, NY.

Selected Poems, edited by Francisco Garcia Lorca & Donald M. Allen. Introduction by W.S. Merwin. Reissued 2006. New Directions pb. 1st printing, 2006. New York, NY.

Lorca/Blackburn. Poems of Federico Garcia Lorca chosen & translated by Paul Blackburn. Momo's Press San Francisco, 1979.

The Gypsy Ballads of Garcia Lorca. Translated by Rolfe Humphries. An Indiana Poetry Paperback. 1953, 3rd Printing. Indiana University Press, Indiana. 3rd Printing, 1963.

A Season In Granada. Uncollected Poems & Prose. Edited and translated by Christopher Maurer. Anvil Press Poetry, pb, 1998, London, England.

Poet In New York- a bilingual edition. Translated by Greg Simon & Steven F. White. Edited by Christopher Maurer. First Edition, 1988. Farar, Straus & Giroux New York, NY.

Poet In New York- Newly Revised and Expanded Bilingual Edition- FSG Classics- Translated from the Spanish by Greg Simon and Steven F. White. Edited & with an introduction & notes by Christopher Maurer. 3rd Edition, 2013. Farar, Straus & Giroux. New York, NY

**Plays**

The House of Bernarda Alba- in a new English version by David Hare. 2005. Faber & Faber, Inc. London, England. pb- Based on a literal translation by Simon Scarfield.

The Public & Play Without a Title. Translated by Carlos Bauer. A New Directions Book, pb, 1978, New York, NY.

Three Tragedies by Lorca Blood Wedding, Yerma & The House of Bernarda Alba. Translated by James Graham- Lujan & Richard L. Connell. Introduction by Francisco

Garcia Lorca. A New Directions Book. pb, First published in 1955. (15th Printing) New Directions Books. New York, NY

### Critical Studies of Federico Garcia- Lorca & Related Reading

Binding, Paul. Lorca- The Gay Imagination. First Published 1985. GMP Publishers Ltd. pb. Criticism & Interpretation.

Campbell, Roy. Federico Garcia Lorca with selected translations of his poetry. 1952. Yale University Press. pb. "An Appreciation of his Poetry".

Cavanough, SSJ; Cecelia J. Lorca's Drawings and Poems: Forming the Eye of the Reader. hc. Associated University Presses. 1995. "Authors as Artists."

Cobb, Carl W. Federico Garcia Lorca. Twayne's World Authors Series. Twayne Publishers. G.K. Hall & Co., Boston, MA. 1967. hc.

Honig, Edwin. Garcia Lorca. A New Directions Paperback Revised Edition, 1963. New Directions, New York & Norfolk, CT.

Johnston, David. Federico Garcia Lorca. Outlines Series. Absolute Press, 1998. Somerset, England & New York, NY. pb..

Kennedy, A.L. on Bullfighting. First Anchor Books Edition, April, 2001. pb. Chapter 3 on Garcia Lorca.

Martinez Naal, Rafael. Federico Garcia Lorca and The Public: A Study of an Unfinished Play and of Love and Death in Lorca's Work. hc. Schocken Books, New York, NY. 1974.

Predmore, Richard L. Lorca's New York Poetry: Social injustice, dark love, lost faith. hc. Duke University Press. Durham, N.C. 1980

### Poems

St. John of the Cross. Translated with an introduction, by Willis Barnstone. New Directions Paperback, New York, NY. 1972.

St. John of The Cross. Selections from The Dark Night & Other Writings. Foreword by Ron Hansen. Edited and with an Introduction by Emilie Griffin. Translation by Kieran Kavanaugh, O.C.D. pb. Harper. San Francisco, CA. First edition, 2004.
St. John of the Cross. Alchemist of the Soul. His Life, His Poetry (Bilingual), His Prose. Foreword by Seyyed Hassein Nasr. Translated with Commentary by Antonio T. de Nicolas. pb. Weiser Books, Boston, MA / York, Beach, ME. 1996.

The Life of Saint Teresa of Avila by Herself. Translated with an Introduction by J.M. Cohen. Penguin Books. pb. 1957. Penguin Classics, Penguin Books, London, England & New York, NY, USA.

### On-line

Re: Eisenberg
Police & Courts: March 19, 2011, Saratoga Springs Police Department,
www.saratogian.com

Lorca and Censorship: The Gay Artist Made Heterosexual
Eisenberg. daniel.eisenberg@bigfoot.com

Patricia Billings
Philip H. Cummings: A work in progress.
www.philipcummings.net/writings.php

Sean Andrew Heaney received his Masters Degree in Poetry from Bennington College on the Jane Kenyon scholarship. He wrote a weekly Poetry column for the Boston Herald and worked on Special Collections at The Boston Public Library. He was librarian at The Boston Ballet School For Dance Education, and has given poetry readings all over New England, New York City & Los Angeles. He was a guest poet at The Vermont Studio Center in Johnson, Vermont. A Vermont native, he now lives in the Northeast Kingdom of Vermont.

www.ingramcontent.com/pod-product-compliance
Lightning Source LLC
Chambersburg PA
CBHW060431050426
42449CB00009B/2246